Nucleus Notions:
Nursery Rhymes Re-imagined

Marcus Anthony Trinder

"Humpty Dumpty":
A Biological Adventure

Humpty Dumpty was a cell,
On a leaf, he did dwell.
With membranes thin and nucleus round,
Life's secrets in him were found.

All the botanists and their mates,
Looked through microscopes, opened gates.
Why did Humpty choose to be here?
'Photosynthesis,' they said clear.

Cells divide and they might merge,
In nature's dance, to life they urge.
Humpty taught us, in his way,
Life's wonders bloom every day.

"Row, Row, Row Your Boat":
A Geographic Expedition

Flow, flow, flow the stream,
Across the lands, where sunbeams gleam.
Mighty mountains, valleys low,
See the world, as you go.

Sail, sail, sail the sea,
From the Arctic, where penguins be.
Deserts hot and forests green,
So many places to be seen.

Turn, turn, turn the globe,
In your room, let it probe.
Every country, big and small,
Geography is the study of all.

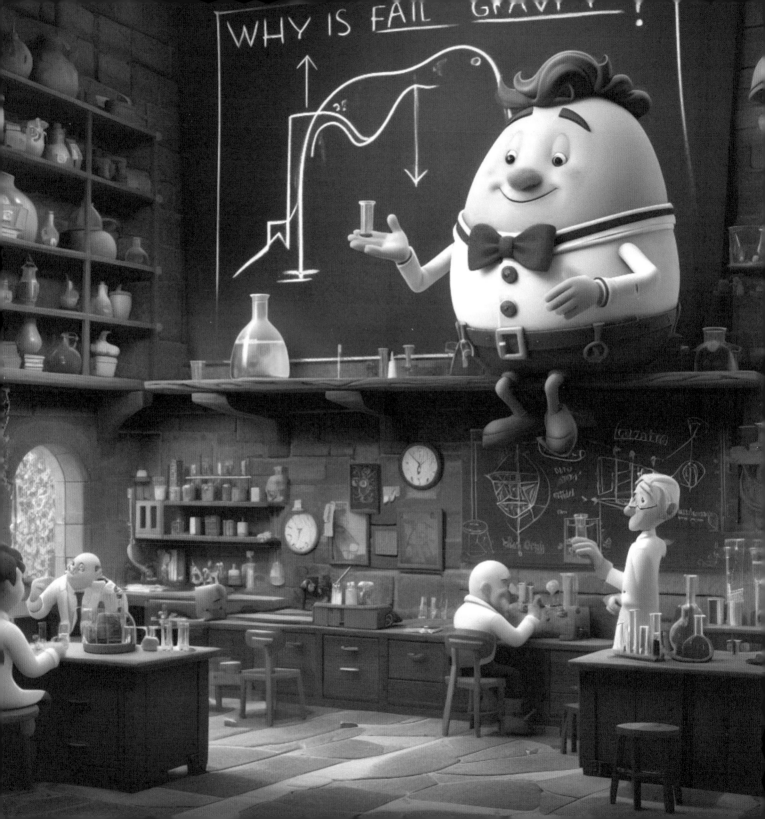

"Humpty Dumpty":
A Hypothesis in Motion

Humpty Dumpty had a notion,
Sat on a wall, with a potion.
He hypothesized it might not fall,
But gravity said, 'I rule all.'

All the scientists and their friends,
Studied the data end to end.
Why did Humpty have a great slide?
'The force of gravity,' they replied.

Experiments may sometimes break,
But from them, knowledge we'll take.
Humpty taught us, on that day,
To test our thoughts in every way.

"Thinker, Thinker, Little Mind": A Glimpse into Philosophy

Thinker, thinker, little mind,
Question all you seek and find.
Up above the world so vast,
Wonder all about our past.

When the thoughts begin to flow,
Question what you think you know.
Dreamer, dreamer, dream so deep,
Ponder mysteries as you sleep.

Why the sky? Why the tree?
Why the buzzing bumblebee?
Seeker, seeker, question why,
Always aim your thoughts so high.

Thinker, thinker, little mind,
Life's big answers you will find.
Learning's more than just a chart,
Start with questions in your heart

"Itsy Bitsy Tortoise":
A Journey Through Evolution

Itsy bitsy tortoise tread,
Through the ages, stories spread.
From dino roars in jungles thick,
To woolly mammoths, ice and slick.

Down came tales from creatures gone,
Fossils, bones, the tale spun on.
Up popped scientists with brushes neat,
Digging up history, all complete.

Itsy bitsy tortoise, slow and wise,
Carrying epochs beneath the skies.
We see in his shell, ages unfold,
Animal tales, waiting to be told.

"Jack and Jill":
Nature's Cycle in Rhyme

Jack and Jill rose with the heat,
Evaporating, quite a feat.
Into the clouds, they turned to rain,
Falling to the earth, over field and lane.

Down as rain, to the ground they fell,
Jack became a stream, as stories tell.
Jill seeped deep, to waters underground,
Quietly moving, without a sound.

Together they met in a river wide,
Flowing, merging with the tide.
Jack and Jill, in the sea they play,
Ready to rise and start another day

"If You're Thoughtful and You Know It": Embracing Emotional Intelligence

If you're curious and you know it, ask a "why?"
Why?
If you're curious and you know it, ask a "why?"
Why?
If you're curious and you know it, and your face will surely show it,
If you're curious and you know it, ask a "why?"
Why?
If you're grateful and you know it, say "thank you."
Thank you!
If you're grateful and you know it, say "thank you."
Thank you!
If you're grateful and you know it, and your smile will surely show it,
If you're grateful and you know it, say "thank you."
Thank you!
If you're puzzled and you know it, scratch your head.
Hmm...
If you're puzzled and you know it, scratch your head.
Hmm...
If you're puzzled and you know it, and your eyes will surely show it,
If you're puzzled and you know it, scratch your head.
Hmm...
If you're mindful and you know it, take a breath.
Inhale... Exhale...
If you're mindful and you know it, take a breath.
Inhale... Exhale...
If you're mindful and you know it, and your calm will surely show it,
If you're mindful and you know it, take a breath.
Inhale... Exhale...

"Old MacDonald Had a Brain": A Journey into the Mind

Old MacDonald had a brain, E-I-E-I-O
And in that brain he found a lobe, E-I-E-I-O
With a think-think here, and a dream-dream there
Here a thought, there a sense, everywhere signals danced
Old MacDonald had a brain, E-I-E-I-O

Old MacDonald had a brain, E-I-E-I-O
And in that brain he found some neurons, E-I-E-I-O
With a zap-zap here, and a zap-zap there
Here a spark, there a pulse, everywhere links made
Old MacDonald had a brain, E-I-E-I-O

Old MacDonald had a brain, E-I-E-I-O
And in that brain he felt emotions, E-I-E-I-O
With a smile-smile here, and a cry-cry there
Here a laugh, there a sigh, everywhere feelings fly
Old MacDonald had a brain, E-I-E-I-O

"Wee Webby Wallace":
The Digital Dilemma

Wee Webby Wallace roams through the net,
Through bytes and bits, where trolls are met;
Scrolling through pages, swiping the screen,
Seeking the good, amidst the mean.

"Limit your time," he often would say,
"Too much screen-time keeps the real world at bay."
With every like, share, and emoji sent,
He reminds, "Real connections are what's meant."

In a world of pings, and endless feeds,
Wallace warns of digital weeds.
"Protect your mind, and guard your heart,
From the web's darker, trickier part."

He's Willie's cousin, from the age of the byte,
Guiding the youth, ensuring they're alright.
When screens allure with their radiant glow,
Remember Wallace's wisdom and take it slow.

For amidst the memes, the games, and the chat,
There's a world outside, don't forget that.
Play in the sun, read a book, take a walk,
Sometimes it's good to just sit and talk.

Grand Old Maker of the Board

The grand old maker of the board,
He had ten LEDs,
He powered them up to the top,
Then down to ground with ease.

And when they were up, they shined so bright,
And when they were down, they dimmed just right,
And when they were only halfway there,
They blinked with patterns, light to rare.

He showed the kids how circuits flow,
With tiny chips that softly glow,
They learned of currents, volts, and more,
With the grand old maker of the board.

Mary had a curious mind

Mary had a curious mind,
A curious mind, a curious mind.
And everywhere that Mary went,
She asked why? and how? and when?

She saw a star up in the sky,
And wondered how it got so high.
She read her books and then she knew,
That fusion made its bright, bold hue.

One day she thought, Why does rain fall?
And so she set to test it all.
With jars outside in sun and shade,
She watched where puddles formed and stayed.

Why does this happen? Mary wrote,
In her bright, bold inquiry note.
She made a guess, then tested more,
Until new knowledge she could store.

Ring Around the Roses, We Plant Seeds Down

Ring around the roses,
Pockets full of posies,
Ashes, ashes,
We plant seeds down.

Watch them in the sunlight,
Growing so tall and bright,
Raindrops, raindrops,
We all see them sprout.

Flowers now are blooming,
Colors are assuming,
Petals, petals,
We see them all spread.

Seasons change, they're wilting,
Back to earth they're tilting,
Cycle, cycle,
We all start again.

Hey Diddle Diddle,
The Stars as Our Riddle

Hey diddle diddle,
The cat and the fiddle,
The cow jumped over the moon,
The little dog laughed to see such sport,
And the dish ran away with the spoon.

Why did the cow jump so high?
Asked a girl with a twinkle in her eye,
Could it escape Earths pull,
And dance with moonbeams in the sky?

Her brother thought and then replied,
Its all about force and mass,
Gravity pulls and objects fall,
But imagine, what a blast!

To rocket ships and Newtons laws,
The girl exclaimed with cheer,
In space and time, there's so much more,
For us to learn and steer.

Hey diddle diddle,
The stars as our riddle,
Well venture far and soon,
With science as our guide tonight,
Well dance beyond the moon.

Little Bo Peep's Celestial Curiosity

Little Bo Peep has lost her sheep,
And can't find where they've been.
But up she looks, to the twinkling books,
Of stars that she's so keen.

Is that a star or planet far?
She asks while gazing light.
Or might it be a ship, on a space-bound trip,
Sailing through the night?

With a telescope near, her vision's clear,
The universe she does sweep.
She sees Saturn's rings and other things,
Its beauty makes her weep.

Little Bo Peep forgot her sheep,
With stars, her heart's in space.
The wonders so vast, from present to past,
Bring joy to her glowing face.

Mary's Quest for Knowledge

Mary had a little lamb,
Its fleece was white as snow;
And everywhere that Mary went,
Shed wonder and she'd go.

Why is its fleece so white? she asked,
And Why does it follow so?
Is it instincts deep, or bonds that keep,
Her lamb wherever she will go?

In class one day, which Mary loved,
She studied cells and genes,
She learned how traits pass parent to child,
In life's grand, wondrous schemes.

DNA, her teacher said,
Makes lambs wool white, not red.
And neurons in its brain, she taught,
Guide it to trot, and not dread.

Now Mary dreams of labs and slides,
And all that she could learn,
Of animals, plants, and microbes too,
At every twist and turn

Ba Ba Black Sheep
and the Mysteries of Metaphysics

Ba ba black sheep, have you any answers?
To questions deep and vast, like ancient seers and dancers.
Metaphysics, a journey of thoughts unexplored,
Let's seek the mysteries, with wonder, we'll be floored.

Ba ba black sheep, what's the nature of time?
Does it flow like a river, or is it more sublime?
In metaphysics, we ponder, as the seconds tick away,
What's the true nature of time? Let's explore today.

Ba ba black sheep, what is real, what is not?
Are our dreams and thoughts, in this world, tightly wrought?
Metaphysical questions, like a puzzle to be solved,
Reality's true nature, let's get involved.

Ba ba black sheep, what's the meaning of it all?
Life's purpose and existence, let's not let it fall.
In metaphysics, we contemplate, as we grow,
The deep, profound questions, that make us wonder so.

So, ba ba black sheep, let's explore, let's inquire,
Metaphysics beckons, like a burning fire.
Engage with the questions, let your young mind unfurl,
In the world of deep thinking, you'll find a precious pearl.

"Holly Humpty":
A Heartfelt Harmony

Holly Humpty sat on a wall,
Feeling emotions, big and small.
When feelings surged, and she almost fell,
She took deep breaths and calmed herself well.

"Know your emotions," Holly would say,
"They come and they go, they don't always stay."
Anger and sadness, joy and surprise,
Holly observed them, wise in her eyes.

When she felt jittery, ready to tumble,
She'd speak to her heart, soft and humble.
"I recognize you," she'd whisper to fear,
"Thanks for the message, but I'm staying right here."

For Holly Humpty, on that tall wall,
Knew self-awareness was the secret for all.
By understanding and feeling each vibe,
She balanced her life, with no need to hide.

The Molecules Joined Two by One

The molecules joined two by one, hoorah! hoorah!
The molecules joined two by one, hoorah! hoorah!
The molecules joined two by one,
Hydrogen met with oxygen,
Water they made with a strong bond then,
And they all flowed into the flask.

The atoms came one by two, eureka! eureka!
The atoms came one by two, eureka! eureka!
The atoms came one by two,
Helium won't bond it's true,
Noble gases, there are a few,
And they all just float so free!.

The ions paired plus and minus, charge! charge!
The ions paired plus and minus, charge! charge!
The ions paired plus and minus,
Sodium met with chloride just,
Together as salt, they stay true,
And they all went into the mix.

The metals shared in a sea, conduct! conduct!
The metals shared in a sea, conduct! conduct!
Electrons move and they flow so free,
Conducting electricity,
some are strong and full with might,
And they all just shine in the light,

The Wheels on the Bus go round and round, But How?

The wheels on the bus go round and round,
Round and round, round and round,
The wheels on the bus go round and round,
But how do they spin so well?

Is it gears, asked a child, that turn them around?
Or is it a motor that makes the sound?
The questions rose as they rode through the town,
As the wheels spun round and round.

The doors on the bus swing open and shut,
Open and shut, open and shut,
The doors on the bus swing open and shut,
But how do they move just right?

Is it hydraulics, thought a girl with a frown,
That lifts them and sets them softly back down?
Her mind filled with questions, as they rode through the town,
While the doors swung open and shut.

The lights on the bus flash on and off,
On and off, on and off,
The lights on the bus flash on and off,
But what makes them blink so bright?

Is it circuits, wondered a boy with a grin,
That manage the current flowing therein?
He pondered and questioned, as their journey begin,
While the lights flashed on and off.

Jack and Logic Hill

Jack and Jill, with minds so keen,
Went up the hill, to think and glean;
Jack posed a riddle, and Jill thought it through,
"If this is true, then that must be too!"

Up Jack got, and said to Jill,
"Logic is a skill, not just uphill;
If rain comes down, then ground gets wet,
If sun shines bright, we'll cast a shadow, bet!"

Jill replied with a thoughtful frown,
"If you jump up, you must come down;
Cause and effect, it's clear to see,
One thing leads to another, logically."

Jack then said, "Here's one for you,
If all birds fly, and sparrows do too;
Then sparrows are birds, it's clear as the sky,
Logical thinking, you can't deny!"

Jill smiled and said, "It's fun to deduce,
With logic and reason, there's no excuse;
For every action, there's a reaction in kind,
With logical thinking, answers we'll find."

This Old Planet

This old planet, number one,
Mercury, closest to the sun;
With a knick-knack paddy-whack,
Orbit round, and circle back,
Mercury's hot and very small.

This old planet, number two,
Venus, with its toxic brew;
With a knick-knack paddy-whack,
Orbit round, without a track,
Venus spins the other way.

This old planet, number three,
Earth, our home, blue and free;
With a knick-knack paddy-whack,
Orbit round, on the right track,
Earth has life and deep blue seas.

This old planet, number four,
Mars, with deserts, myths, and more;
With a knick-knack paddy-whack,
Orbit round, and leave a track,
Mars has rovers exploring its floor.

This old planet, number five,
Jupiter, where storms thrive;
With a knick-knack paddy-whack,
Orbit round, with a big pack,
Jupiter's moons, sixty-nine alive!

...

···

This old planet, number six,
Saturn, with its icy tricks;
With a knick-knack paddy-whack,
Orbit round, with ringed flack,
Saturn shines with beautiful mix.

This old planet, number seven,
Uranus, tilted up to heaven;
With a knick-knack paddy-whack,
Orbit round, on a side track,
Uranus spins in a topsy-fashion.

This old planet, number eight,
Neptune, with winds that don't abate;
With a knick-knack paddy-whack,
Orbit round, in the distant black,
Neptune's storms are truly great.

This old dwarf, once number nine,
Pluto, on the edge, still looking fine;
With a knick-knack paddy-whack,
It's not a planet, let's not flack,
Pluto's heart still brightly shines.

Everly Cleverly Crow:
Always A Thought Ahead

The clever little crow flew up to the sky,
Wanting to reach the clouds so high.
Rain came down, and blocked its way,
But the crow just smiled, not led astray.

It found a tool, used it just right,
And soon the problem was out of sight.
Up it soared, above the trees,
Adapting, learning, with such ease.

The clever little crow, faced challenge anew,
But it thought and thought, and then it knew!
For every twist, turn, high and low,
The crow found a way, putting on a show.

So when things get tough, as they sometimes will,
Remember the crow, and its extraordinary skill.
Face your problems, think them through,
And just like the crow, you'll know what to do!

Three States of Matter

Three kinds of matter,
See how they change,
From solid to liquid,
And then to a range,

First there's the solid,
Like ice or a stone,
It holds its shape,
Stands firm and alone,

Then comes the liquid,
Like water or tea,
It flows and it pours,
Moves so freely,

Lastly, the gas,
Like air or steam,
It fills up the space,
Invisible it seems,

Three kinds of matter,
From Earth to the skies,
Learn and discover,
Open your eyes!

In My Mind, What Do I See?

In my mind, what do I see?
Thoughts and dreams, all part of me.
Colors, sounds, feelings so deep,
Are they just dreams or thoughts that leap?

The robot walks, the robot talks,
But can it feel the way a bird squawks?
Is it just wires, circuits, and gears?
Or can it know joys, hopes, and fears?

The sun does rise, the moon does set,
But do they think, or feel regret?
Are we all like a winding clock?
Moving to a tick and tock?

In our minds, so vast and wide,
Questions linger, side by side.
Is feeling real, or just a play?
Of atoms dancing, night and day?

So ponder deep, and wonder why,
Our minds can think, feel, and fly.
The answers might be far and wide,
But seek, and let your thoughts be your guide.

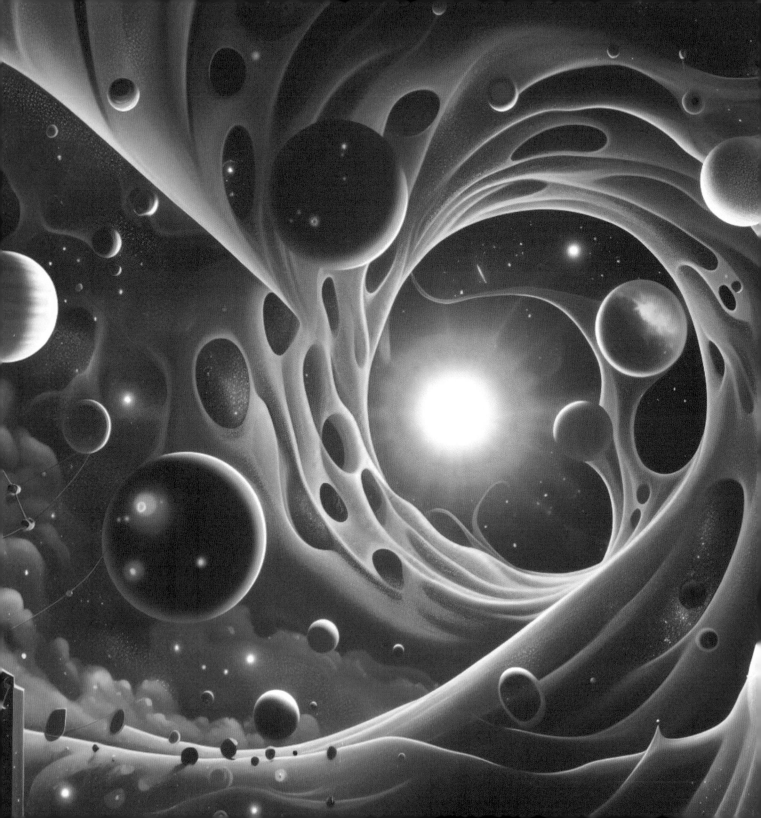

Ponder, Ponder, Vast Expanse

Ponder, ponder, vast expanse,
How you make the dreamers dance;
Up above the world so high,
Secrets held in the night sky,

Glistening lights, so far away,
Galaxies where mysteries lay;
Atoms, quarks, and black hole seams,
Holding universe's dreams,

Ponder, ponder, vast expanse,
Philosophy and science's chance;
Why are we, and what is time?
Universe's rhythmic rhyme,

Ponder, ponder, thoughts so deep,
Questions that our minds will keep;
Curiosity, our guiding star,
Leading us, both near and far.

**Keep thinking,
Keep dreaming,
Keep doing!**

Printed in Great Britain
by Amazon